Little Angels

Alex Chornyj

My name is Alex Chornyj, I am a reiki master teacher and as such my writing reflects the energy and light that surrounds my spirit. One who realizes their potential and purpose by developing their creative calling will be successful in their endeavour to reinvigorate the life force which is central to all of our spirits. I listen to my heart that speaks through my soul embracing the life within encapsulating the life without in a oneness leading to an inner peace. I am continually evolving physically, mentally, spiritually, emotionally and etherically in an upward ascendance towards a greater enlightenment. I have been published in The Canadian Federation Of Poetry, Poetry Super Highway, Touch Magazine in England, Decanto Magazine in England, Fashion For Collapse Magazine,I Speak Project, Awaken Consciousness Magazine, Earthborne Magazine, Gloom Cupboard Magazine,The Not Magazine, The Tower Journal, White Mountain Publications, and 2Sloitudes Magazine in Montreal as well as a host of others. I have been writing for approximately forty years and my inspiration is derived through my spirit guides. When I do public readings I often receive responses how my voice inflection carries a vibrational frequency that touches heart chakras in a soothing and calming manner. This binding of thoughts was manifested as a collaboration of an esoteric synthesis.

Contents

Little Angels Dust Your Wings

Little angels dust your wings
Close your eyes softly
It's time to sleep
The forest is quiet.
Morning is a ways off
Settle down in your tiny bed
Let your dreams take you to a place
That is as peaceful,
As it is pristine
For life begins its enchantment
You have done your day's good deeds
Here are your many returns.
As one good turn
Deserves another
A reciprocal two way street
Is what you are part of.
You touch lives in a manner
As you go about your day
You sprinkle rays of sunshine
You make the hardest look inward.
You help many find
What was never lost
Just covered over by a frost
That melts in your presence.
As you traipse across a field
You leave behind in its wake
A thought that takes root
Spiralling into one's consciousness.
The world as we know it

Has you to thank
For bringing into being
A reason to reach for tomorrow.
As night sees you resting
You are one step ahead
Endowing life with a tranquil calm
Seeing your surroundings glisten.
So sleep, gently sleep
Let your soul drift near and far
What you find in your travels
You transmit to morning's sunrise.

Cherishing Affections

You have reached your resting oasis
Can take solace in knowing
The torch for one
Is still burning brightly.
You have earned your quiet space
In your landscape of sunsets
As you are your own maker
So control these hands of time.
Can go as slow
Or as fast as you desire
You're at the helm
Of a ship you navigate.
So off into the blue yonder
Does the wind take to your sails
You can listen
To your heart's content.
As this is your transition
Whose current follows your lead
A year has passed
Since your elevation.
As you're now upon a lake
That holds this enchanted peace
In such comes a freedom
Which lets your spirit soar so high.
And so you remember
The talks we use to share
About what's on the other side
How communication lines stay open.
For as long as you're able to

I'll be where you know I am
As love has no abrogation
I shall forever be your son.
So when you see a ripple
You know it's me sending thoughts
Ones that still make you smile
As your tears of joy seed our clouds,
With a warming embrace
For your arms still cross over
In the form of a sprinkle
With fingers of cherishing affections.

Tide

I want to grow old together
To be with you constantly
Part of each sunrise
To share in the miracle,
That we so are
For we have been blessed
I am of the belief
We are here for a reason.
One that reveals itself
More to us each day
In so many ways
As our life is an orchard.
We bear the fruits
Amongst all the trees
A sweetness whose residue
Resonates deep within.
For we're as eternal
As the earth and sky
Being of the light
A shine that follows,
Us endlessly
Painting our shadows
With transcendental hues
Across an infinite path.
That we traverse
As two spirits intertwined
In a coherent array
Moving in simultaneous,
Even synchronistic patterns

As we're on the same page
Close to the mark
Whose chart we emulate.
Like an ensemble
As two of a sound
That finely permeates
In and around the universe.
This plays on a tune
That we keep inside
An echo that shimmers
On a smooth sailing tide.

Effervescence

We tied a knot
With one thread from each other
As a vow we gave
Never to forsake a trust.
In for the long haul
Sweet, just not short
From first I held your hand
Still tingling to this day.
To me is a sign
We did something right
So well in fact
Why we've gained a permanence.
Is etched and entrenched
Within our seams
In my every breath
In our hopes and dreams.
Where do we go from here ?
To the outer reaches
So far, yet so close
As we're joined in the heart.
No matter if apart
Are always near
I take you with me
To comfort my soul.
Through thick and thin
As knowing that you're there
Is all that I need
To persevere.
Call this what you will

A steadying influence
A marked improvement
Since you entered my life.
I haven't been the same
With you I've touched the stars
Every single twinkle
Whose sparkles have us endowed,
With a glowing warmth
That even in
The most frigid cold
These embers kindle an enamoured effervescence.

Regeneration Of Souls

The smoke is billowing
The trees and plant life
Leave their cries to the wind
To echo across the currents.
The nights are sheer desperation
Where is the one ?
To place the turquoise in the water
To bring the soothing rains.
The land is being scorched
Temperatures have risen
To create a tinder box
Due to lightning or careless humans.
The earth feels like
The surface of the sun
Animals flee the peril instinctively
With their hearts barely intact.
These voices congregate
One has heard their pleas
His soul aches from this demise
Such trembling shakes the land.
From ocean to ocean
His tears begin to glow
He walks in a forest
Untouched, but still bewildered.
As he comes to a river
With emerald hues
He places his chain of stones
With deliberate intent.
As clouds begin to form

Whose distance is a world away
Yet his spirit experiences
The anguish like he was one of them.
Raindrops start to fall
One after the other
Then in sheets and streams
A calm overcomes the acrid suffocation.
Gentle hands caress
Sweeping ever so gracefully
As tiny saplings find daylight
So does a regeneration of souls reincarnate.

Distant Ring

Distant ring of the drums
Heard throughout the valley
When the river ran its course
Full of abundance.
Took what one needed
Enough berries from a plant
Fruit from a tree
When man and earth were one.
All part of creation
The cry of the wolf
From top of the canyon
Struck not fear, but courage.
Learned to watch the brown bear
As if you they nurtured
You were like their child
You grew with that footprint.
For what you absorbed then
Would one day pass on
To little ones you would have
Was the nature of life.
Your ears don't fail you
Hear crackle of the fire
Sinters rise in the darkness
Like firefly wisping about.
Only now realize
None of these memories
Are from your current path
But one you once walked.
Your hands work in a way

You never knew they could
Flow in a motion
Fluent with symbols.
You have not forgotten
Dreams are a reminder
Of a simpler time
Replace torn pages in a book.
Feel drum's vibration
Entered, never left
Stayed within confines of your soul
A soul that is ageless.

Speaking Symbols

A temple in the sky
Higher than the tallest clouds
Topped with virgin snows
In a mystical vision.
To appear out of nowhere
As there, spirits dwell
Silently upon the winds
Until this volcano awakens.
On this day she was dormant
Her beauty picturesque
A majestic immortality
In vibrant vibrations.
Of regal nature
As this crown so wears
With dignity, distinction
In a timeless capsule.
A world within worlds
A life inside a life
To capture for a moment
To remain in memory forever.
Etched in an endless array
To come forth in dreams
To stand on its own
In line with a chain,
That forged a continent
Of which she was part
From lands of molten rock
Whose heights protrude through,
White floating mists

Revealing ancient paths
As they follow in the distance
In carved antiquity.
Of this I had a glimpse
A treasure to keep
With its vividness
That can still a heartbeat.
Adorned by crossing currents
These swirls swiftly meet
Creating lines of lineage
To remember in speaking symbols.

Scars Of A Generation

We were under siege
From a wave of intolerance
So searched for safe haven
Due to our cultural ethnicity.
Seen by those as the weaker race
Protected by no conventions
Left to fend for ourselves
By ones who'd put us asunder.
The days of war
The trials that ensued
The heartache and tears
Lives lost in searing dungeons.
A hunted people
From an unfounded hatred
With the intention
Of complete annihilation.
Instincts unknown
Until facing this enemy
We as a nationality
A tormented friction.
Lines of persecutions
Rivers of boiled blood
Buried as corpses
In holes of forgotten memories.
Pockets of resistance
Keeping to a silence
Unless uncovered
Due to some betrayal.

Hoping beyond hope
This was all a bad nightmare
Waking to the reality
The impossibility,
Of an enduring invisibility
Like pages in a book
Crumpled before their time
Lessons learned lasting longer than life.
The scars of a generation
The remnants and residues
Linger and languishing to this day
Reminders of a history not to repeat.

Dignity

Do you really know me ?
You think I have no mind
I've retained this faculty
Can empathy you find ?
I am paralyzed
But I still have my dignity
You've not yet realized
I do speak coherently.
You treat me like I'm not there
I just need a friend
One who will some time share
With me before my life does end.
Things need not be repeated
As I still have my memory
That's why I get frustrated
I am not a baby.
I like to be independent
As much as I can
What I have is permanent
I know I'm a sick man.
But I still want to live
Please close me in no closet
I have so much to give
What I learned I didn't forget.
Your smile brightens my day,
Your touch on my shoulder
Gives the warmth that may
Help me live a while longer.
I know your job's not easy

In it is much stress
I want to be no burden to thee
I wish myself I could dress.
I know my limitations
That it'd take a miracle
Unrealistic expectations
To walk I'll never be able.
But that doesn't mean
That I can't be happy
For this I have been
Since you came to listen to me.

Higher Branches

I've seen things you have not
You've seen things I have not
As one we see clearer
With you higher branches appear.
We've caused a chain reaction
A tree in hibernation
Has come out of its sleep
To us, each day will be like spring.
Our earth once more stirs
Life signs we detect
Which are universal in scope
Romance returns to a once sullen ground.
We know what we represent
Meaning of our being here
By this very virtue
Islands are again on the move.
What was a damper on things
Has had its lid removed
So air and sun combine
To let the earth again breathe.
This lid had kept us apart
Like an invisible partition
Which melts away like the snow
For determination overcame isolation.
The ground beneath our feet
Softens by a gentle rain
Saplings push upwards
As do trees with hollow centers.
With you I gain insight

With me you feel the pulse of the moon
We reach for the next limb
Which radiates with a renewed vigour.
We absorb wisdom wisely
Lines of communication
Re-establish a mentality
Through an inner rhythm.
Bodies feel lighter
The higher we ascend
For the maze has been replaced
As we enter our domain.

Sentient Wisdom

Can't plan too far ahead
As the gaps left in between
Are more than giant leaps
They become unrealistic goals.
Don't want to look way down
For you may get vertigo
By slow, methodical steps
So retain an integrity.
If spread too thin
There is a danger
Of slipping inside the cracks
The task is to stay current.
Not to be lost
In a time warp
For once initiated
There's no end in sight.
As a clock's hands
Must pass by in seconds
Not the speed of light
Or else your voice,
Is then like a fly on the wall
Indecipherable
To be able to interpret
Requires a calm exchange.
To be meaningful
One so thinks in terms
Of a horse before the cart
Of a life in stages.
Not as a competition

Or a race against oneself
As much can be said
For being last, but cognizant.
And in one piece
By keeping intact
You live to see another day
To put this all together,
In its totality
To realize a purpose
To experience first hand
A sentient wisdom.

Moment In Time

To stand where you are
Looking out across this lake
Thinking is there someone else ?
Peering back from the other side.
As these waters go on
What seem like forever
No word of a lie
In all directions,
You are humbled
Not only being here
At this moment in time
But to be in the presence,
Of that which you stirs
To be with the dawn
To breathe in a breeze
So sets your eyes ablaze.
As big as the moon
Which stares you right in the face
Hanging inches above
So close that this orb,
You think you can touch
Then when you try
You tend to make a splash
In these laughing waves.
Which get quite a chuckle
From your innocent demise
A harmless rendition
Of a helpless duck.
When you get back on land

Raining endless
Dripping,dabbing drops
Hard to reclaim,
Some sort of seriousness
In a solemn attempt
Then once more mesmerized
By a roundness in the sky.
Then you hear an echo
In soft ripples
An enchanting voice
But there's no mermaid in sight.

Morning Sky

I'm on my way home
To be back in the arms
Of the tender mother
Who brought me in this world.
The time is near
As the candle that burns
Finishes its rotation
Which is my signal,
To be gone from this place
How do I say goodbye ?
To those who've walked with me
I will remember fondly.
As these memories
Will stay intact
A piece of my heart
Is embedded,
Into each one of them
Life has been a journey
As many roads
Have I travelled.
I've had close calls
I've lived my dreams
As I now come face to face
With my own mortality.
I have no regrets
As I have done
What I wanted to do
With an exuberance.
I wouldn't change a thing

If I had to do this
All over again
As I like being on the edge.
Please don't feel sorry
I don't want sympathy
Just a celebration
Of who I am.
Smile and be happy
The apple of my eye
The twinkle from the laughter
As I drift upon a morning sky.

Spirit Side Of Existence

I would have liked
To stay a while longer
But what first brought me here
Said the last crystal,
Has left my hour glass
When your time is up
There is no bargaining
Just acceptance,
Of one's own fate
As I am at peace with myself
I know this story continues
Just on a new page.
This does not mean
I move on without
My treasured memories
Love has no boundaries.
It dwells in all realms
As you still think of me
A part of my heart
Will yet be on the earth plane.
My dear family
Please see this as a blessing
Let this sun cross our paths
Remember my smile,
With joy, not sadness
As I see you from where I am
With a cherished tenderness
Which spans the distance between.
To create a bridge

One that will stand
The test of time
With mom I'll be waiting.
To welcome you with open arms
A place is set aside
As was mine with my passing
The spirit side of existence.
Is as real as the footsteps
Which I used to take
Now I'm lighter on my feet
Even more the person you once warmly embraced.

Congruent Waters

If you don't try
You'll never know
What could have been
What lies beneath,
This unrealized square block
If the ground stays
Quiet, undisturbed
This won't craft the unknown.
As who and what you are
So embedded deep within
Will this way remain
As a withheld secret,
Unless there is passion
A movement afoot
That will work its magic
In revealing qualities.
Then and only then
Will flat edges be rounded
As an etched surface
Begins to take shape.
Each line being a thought
As words are spoken
Angles of accentuation
Create an intricacy.
As to a face
Comes a purpose
A reason to be
As what was empty,
Is slowly filled

With an enduring substance
Of an endearing character
Who has come of age.
The voice is attached
To the person
So becomes refined
By each passing piece,
From a transcended inflection
This maturation
Gives life to a stillness
To a convergence of congruent waters.

Deep Within

You have been in my heart
Long ago touched my soul
When we were two
From one feather.
Then in a canyon
Where we dwelled in harmony
Soaring to a fro
Side by side, eye to eye.
The days were filled
With a fired passion
No end in sight
Just courage in our destiny.
A time of vigour
A pronounced pronunciation
In emphatic images
Of truth and daring.
We lived on currents
In between the spans
Of resuscitating winds
Which lengthened our lines.
Our instincts were honed
We loved and were loved
Showing an undying respect
For the life in which we lived.
We had our faults
But we were humble
To learn from our mistakes
To feel with a sensitivity.
We were at our best

When in the company
Of the other
Together we did flourish.
How vivid are these memories
I can still hear the splash
From dives into crystal waters
Then drying in a warming sun.
Such was the splendour
Of a time etched in our spirits
Shrill calls that struck as a drum
Whose beats yet remain deep within.

Nearing Point

Went back to the forest
To where it all began
I found a slender cave
One I never knew was there.
I had my favourite spots
That were off the beaten path
Which is where I liked to go
Still on this day,
A sliver became visible
One that added to
My repertoire of knowledge
Not by stumbling upon,
Nor by accident
As each piece has its time
When to be revealed
Not before or after.
So as it was
At this fateful moment
When I entered a domain
That was my next step.
I felt an instant
Poignant recognition
Not just of this
Ancient existence,
But of a calmness
A nearing point
From a sacred ground
Of profound emanations.
For here I was struck

By a pure radiance
Each symbol with its meaning
Created a hieroglyphic key.
When turned in its motion
So then was I bestowed
With an inclination
That led to a comprehension.
A venerable venue
Of peaceful prominence
Where I was able to listen
Then absorb an imbibing sentience.

Life Of Spirit

Love, to empty a void
So a chamber can be filled
With unconditional passion
To share songs of the birds.
To hear a music
As sweet as any nectar
Living in the moment
Touching a lasting beauty.
To go without
Ego, jealousy or fear
Is to have a life of spirit
To walk unencumbered.
From this comes compassion
To think beyond oneself
To dwell in a happiness
A place of tranquillity.
To ascend above
The bonds of one circle
To expand into realms
Where we find cognizance.
To not just listen
But absorb with open arms
To embrace emotions
That transcend our comprehension.
As our eyes become another's
One who is less fortunate
To raise them up
To feel the light of the sun.
Then release these rays

To let them flow in a stream
Where all are equals
As each has significance.
To realize our reason
Why we're here at this time
To learn a lesson
Centered in a humbleness.
To be eternally grateful
For all who cross our path
So these shades of colour
Brighten the striations that shimmer in our sky.

Placid Stream

If I had one wish
That I knew would come true
It would be for a universal lasting peace
Throughout all dimensions.
With a ubiquitous permeation
To be here for selah
Not one time crystal less
But an entire encapsulation.
For the betterment of all species
On every world known and unknown
So that a rhythm becomes
Slow and steady as she goes.
This is what I envision
A call to dismantle
To deal with issues
Without anger or hatred.
With a genuine concern
For a greater good
That can be had by all
When a focus is outside the box.
To take into consideration
Possibilities as infinite
As the drops in an ocean
But to be aware,
Of each and every one
In a state of harmony
Each working in conjunction
With, not against,
The one who is beside them

Such is a concept
In the realm of consensus
Where friction is replaced,
By a smooth transition
Down come fences of barb wire
Restored is an open plain
Where wild horses roam free.
It's moving forward
But also taking that from the past
Which is of a purity
Then together finding a placid stream.

Constant Springs

The vision was painted
Up in the dimming sky
Which had enough light
With a rose tinge on its edges,
To show us again
What the future holds
On the wings of a dragon
Who first brought us an omen.
Of a little one we would have
This time though, the image
Was of a young woman
Ready to set the world with beauty.
To restore what has been lost
So earth, air and waters
Can rejuvenate
What a calling is her name, Luna.
She who brings life forces
Together in a circle
One that won't be broken
But kept sacred by an accord.
So her early steps have been
Beset by lesson after lesson
To prepare her for adversity
As there will be those,
Who wish this not to happen
So this is not for the faint of heart
But one with a will
That shall prevail.
So the words now uttered

Must be touched by the brushes
The gentle flowing ones of her soul
As these currents combine,
So emerges the love
Which has been overshadowed
Yet the sun is ready
To do its part.
To fill the skies with music
That from her sweet voice
When she sings with a spirit
That ushers in constant springs.

Windows Of Promise

How two worlds become aligned
Coming from opposite directions
To end up side by side
As windows of promise,
Placing us together
If only for a short time
But it's what transpires
While inside this space,
That leaves both changed forever
As such occurred
By a higher intervention
Which set this synchronicity,
In its designed motion
To create an interaction
One with an indelible mark
Each will keep close to their soul.
For a light so shone
Which will always shine
From day through night
From year to year.
To go forward with
As friends within
An auspicious beam
Whose stream is eternal.
To dwell, to inspire
More of the same
To open a channel
From which flows continuity.
To share in a dawn

That rises each morning
With a belief in knowing
What exists with this sun.
That being a warmth
One that shows where to be
And how to exact a sincerity
Which brings hope to the spirit.
This is the beginning
To what has commenced
Such comes in the distance
Whose nearing is nurtured by illumination.

Crackling Embers

I remember the fun I shared
With my sisters over the years
In the soft, puffy snow
Which now I cherish,
With my wife and daughter
The giggles and smiles
The near wipeouts
Our ecstatic, rosy faces.
How fast we slide
Down the slippery hills
Weaving and winding
Whistling a merry tune.
There we are in our glory
Living in the moment
Creating memorable memories
That will stay with us forever.
The return to the house
To hot chocolate and marshmallows
Snuggling up on the couch
Watching old movies,
Filled with sleigh bells
This is the advent
Of the tingling season
When thoughts center around,
The bridging of differences
The warming of chilling colds
Songs of tenderness
Hugs with no release.
These are what we

Hold dear in our hearts
The time spent in the presence
Of ones in our family tree.
Our blue spruce springs
In its youthful abundance
Thickening and rising
With our glowing gratitude.
Making these traditions
Which become our heritage
A love that wraps us closely
Within its bond of crackling embers.

Immortal Strings

In the land of those
Who are remembered
Names stay attached
Faces retain their images.
Time does not erase lines
The details are enhanced
By living a love
Strengthened in the moment.
Words to go by
That don't lose their intention
No matter the gravity
Are bonds which can't be broken.
As these transcend
Invisible borders
Without expiration
Into perpetuity.
Then we are the totality
Of all that we've ever done
It's not just one revolution
But a series,
Of complementing circles
A start with no finish line
Like rings on a tree
Each being a full life.
When a memory
Is thought of in a way
An ember grows brighter
From this reminiscing.
The simple act

Of smiling at a picture
Is enough to trigger
An enduring response.
To almost travel
Back in time where
We were as children
Passages that create harmony.
Then bringing this forward
To present day
This lingering effect
Forms immortal strings.

Matriarch

Woman who touched us all
Gave without asking
Helped when we would fall
When inside we were aching.
Her cure of brandy
To rid a bad cold
Her sweet macaroni
Which never got old.
Her generosity
Second to none
A woman, a lady
In all, number one.
She lived a good hard life
Strong constitution
Through bliss and strife
She raised three children.
Her love is a symbol
For all to emulate
Her spirit does us humble
Through all reverberates.
Now heard as an echo
She's found her valley
Devoid of sorrow
Filled with serenity.
There she shall remain
There to spread her wings
There, through sun and rain
There, her soul shall sing.
So she now passes

To the next existence
To the next horizon
To a place that her complements.

Continuity

Shades of an existence
Parallels between each one
How they lead into another
To make a continuity of linkages.
As life is round, not flat
There is no drop off
Where endings and beginnings merge
So seamless streams are aligned.
We move across membranes
As akin to travelling
Through states or provinces
Each has its own traits.
But there's no abrogation
Air is here all the way along
As we assume different
Life forms and shapes.
We have constant appearances
Upon many stages
As there's more than one dimension
With the possibility of other universes.
As in spirit we've no restrictions
All borders are invisible
There are no papers to sign
So recognized by your ethereal imprint.
As no matter who you are
You retain what you always had
As your memory is an instrument
To play all kinds of music.
Which bears the fruits

Of an active consciousness
So remembers every place you have been
All you've ever accomplished.
Which is not forgotten
Just because you enter transition
As the paths one walks
Are recorded in sequence,
In the order in which they came
By doing a past life regression
You can follow the phases of your moon
From inception to the present.

Nearing Tunnel

Once more tears come from my eyes
I knew I was not alone
I said a few words
In front of your picture,
Then I felt you both encircle me
With a ring of incandescence
Which put me eternally at peace
From the glow of your endearing warmth.
That left an impression
From this gentle embrace
So formed a breathing rainbow
Whose striations became my air within.
I was comforted
As loving you two the way I do
Your absence still
Makes my heart grow fonder.
An unexpected visit
Only serves to affirm
What I express each day
That your leaving is not cause to say goodbye,
And what dwells between us
Is constantly being sent
In a cycle of reciprocity
Why this circuit prevails.
To be pristine and preserved
Like a river fed by a glacier
Our touch has only been enhanced
A star's glistening is closer.
It is such a sign

That in this evolved plane
There is no isolation
As higher sensitivities come into play.
This kind of contact
Will become more frequent
With a line cleansed and purified
That will encourage these interactions.
As was the case this morning
As emotions enable transparency
To bridge any gap
So places us in a nearing tunnel.

Blossom Under Sunshine

The coming horizon
Is more beautiful than the last
Each one in succession
Has its own unique inclusions.
As inside of these orbs
Are living and conscious entities
Who exist for karmic reasons
To help those find their purpose,
In such a way
So is revealed this potential
That without an initial nudge
Might not ever,
Have been released from their shell
But from these growing crystal spheres
An inspiration is derived
To first move one's limbs,
Then to become adept
Through use of these hemispheres
Which blossom under sunshine
To magnify this brilliance.
Hence why their resonance
Moves into such vibrant shades
Causing an increase in the velocity
Of the spinning shimmers.
As it's not by coincidence
For every action
Has an equal and opposite reaction
As forces of nature,
Dictate natural laws

Ones that as time goes by
Display an autonomous fashion
Particulars that characterize their formations.
The world is seen
Through the eyes of the beholder
My vision is multi-dimensional
Whose depths articulate fascinating fathoms.
From these perceptions
Creativity springs to life
In ethereal emanations
Whose vibrations carve such magical wonders.

"Loving Acceptance"

Come to where I am
It is time for us again
You visit me on the other side
A happiness meets us in the middle.
My winter has been long
When together we shall be
So will the advent of Spring
For you are a warm, caressing breeze.
You looked at our pictures
Of our endless embrace
So yearned for my fingers
I heard your call in the night.
You thought of me
So I shone on you
Your love dreamed of mine
So my heart opened its petals.
I heard no robins
Until your voice so sweet
Brought the essence of this creation
To my wanting, waiting ears.
Mom it was your window
Of your choosing, not our's
These doors will always stay open
More than slightly ajar.
You are beautiful
A sparkling, glowing streak
That will now and forever
Spread itself across our blue skies.
Your emerald eyes

That angelic inflection
Is the cause of inspiration
To paint our lives with your rainbow.
One we'll keep close inside
With the memory of your touch
Of your gentle, serene songs
Whose rhythms will endure,
As does this flowing peace
For to us you are our strength
A faith that conquers fear
To fill us with a loving acceptance.

Light And Resplendence

They're real if you
Just let them be
As we exist
In multiple spheres.
Of which this is but one
These are not myths
Relations of the dragonfly
Or dainty wisps.
Why when in the woods
You feel with instincts
You don't quite trust
Although adept,
In the unknown
Occurrences
You have in the rain
Whose drops open portals.
Through which appear
These magical beings
Not from your sub-conscious
But tunnels of creation.
As parallel universes
Other worlds near and far
Are of a vast array
Of light and resplendence.
We are as different
To them as they are to us
All come from somewhere
Just look at the twinkles,
At night from above

Life in its magnificence
Happens in all corners
Not just the one where you are.
Do not disbelieve
Before you've had a chance
To see for yourself
What shining rays reveal.
When you come upon
The remarkable
Don't look the other way
But embrace with pronunciation.

Through The Ages

I will love you forever
Rains and sunshine will this amplify
Winds and thunder shall us caress
As the earth and sky do us adore.
There are no goodbyes
Only ring after ring
Each life is a page in a book
Once filled, so start one more.
On shelf upon shelf
From which comes a pattern
Of eternal kindness
Of a sight that permeates,
A deepening echo
One that stretches
Farther than the eye can see
That can be heard through the ages.
Why we share this sense
In other lives we've simultaneously
Been a relation to each other
Not always on the same footing.
But with an equal tenderness
This closeness has expanded
Into all parts of our atmospheres
Why we haven't lost touch.
As no matter where you are
I shall still be within range
Due to the strength
Of our beckoning polarity.
Which by each phase is enhanced

As a symbol this morning
Was the thin sliver of moon
Though small, still radiating brightly.
So as we evolve
Yes we both will adapt
To a changing bond
To a life even more enriching.
So every step of the way
Will your presence I feel
Here, there, anywhere
Due to this warmth that is your signature.

Heart Warming Breeze

They know you're coming
The time is almost upon us
An old growth forest you awaits
With sweet cedar when you enter.
You are one of them
And your presence signifies
As does the advent of spring
A renewing of ancient acquaintances.
As the day presents itself
Your journey has watchers
Who provide safe passage
For you and your loved ones.
As you're part of the family
So do you return to a haven
Where you have a rightful place
Inside a ring of reciprocity.
For your's is a venturing spirit
You travel far and often
So are you the culmination
Of these infinite pastures.
Like some droplets
Congregating on a leaf
Each one merging into a circle
Of ubiquitous sage.
Which is what transmits
From a serene plateau
Reaching you way in the distance
With its channelling sinews.
Whose message you absorb

With its corresponding emotion
For the air is alive
In cosmic arrays.
As you near these grounds
There's an abundance of glitter
Sounds emanating
Into your field of awareness,
Are of chords of music
As songbirds align along branches
Whistling and singing
Upon a heart warming breeze.

Stillness

In the calm stillness
Those fingers touch my palm
I fall back into nothingness
I float on the wings of a bird.
I am content
As a dolphin in an ocean
Or a woodpecker
Tapping a tree for sustenance.
Although I take up
Very little space
I'm as yet significant
In what I think and do.
I drift upon a cloud
Here, there, where I'm destined
I breathe deeply, effortlessly
I dream with a child's imagination.
I embrace change
I'm not a stick in the mud
But a branch in a stream
Whose flow is guided by my current.
I am part of all that is
Of those who came before me
Of those who'll come after
Of the mountains,
That rise and fall
Of the silence in my spirit
Of emerald waters
Of ancient songs,
Sung around talking fires

All of which are intertwined
For each life is a step
And at this elevation,
I can place myself
In a meditative state
With a vision of happiness
From an aspiring thought.
So I'm standing in a waterfall
Eyes closed, pulsations bubbling
Gentle gyrations
Nurture a slowing rhythm.

In Time

All things do change
For time does go on
Which might seem strange
But yesterday's gone.
As we get older
We grow more each stage
And become much wiser
With our age.
So now you know
If only a portion
Of why this is so
For life is transition.

Mystical Monarchs

I was born a dragonfly
As my transparent wings
Are as invisible
As a breath of air.
I love skimming over streams
And all those shiny stones
As it seems all that I touch
Undergoes a transformation.
I can zip here and there
Almost turn on a dime
As my smallness
Allows me to manoeuvre smartly.
Fragrances of flowers
Are to me like dawning beacons
For each I decipher
To their purpose and brilliance.
I find them or they find me
Or we discover each other
In this natural menagerie
Of mystical monarchs.
Such is this land
In which I dwell
Of milk and honey
Of proverbial pristineness.
For I am in my glory
As happy go lucky
As I can possibly be
In the midst of miracles.
I dangle on a soft breeze

Almost bobbing up and down
On a whim I travel
From here to there, then everywhere.
I'm in a constant state
Of fluctuation
As I blend with backgrounds
Of aspiring aspirations.
For blossoms are bulging
In blanketing bundles
I'm drawn by intuition
To centres with undulating nectar accents.

Long Points

As twilight came upon my consciousness
My room was filled with silence
Scintillations came streaming through
With them came a kindness.
Asking me to remember
Back when time was rippling
Under a crescent moon
In a meandering forest.
Where there was this lake
A place with a gathering
Of all the long points
Of which I was one.
As I felt this closeness
A nearing I'd envisioned
As this was the culmination
Of my elucidating dreams.
For I was being beckoned
To complete this circle
As a window had once more opened
To envelop rekindling shadows.
For unicorns were appearing
One by one in succession
My spiritual essence
Had its spot oscillating.
The tunnel I was in
Was ever so colourful
I could see far below
A radiance surrounding.
A glowing pulsation

Which was equal to mine
And each one of their's
So came my metamorphosis.
For as I entered this sphere
I could name each one of them
This turquoise light
Flowed from its center.
Our thoughts held this creation
From a circulating effervescence
Touching us all simultaneously
As our paths aligned along a parallel plain.

Deeper Fathoms

As I poked my head out of the sand
I felt my hard shell
And tiny legs moving so fast
In a race to reach the sea.
This survival instinct
Told me what I needed to know
That this was going
To be a journey,
With a lot of darting about
Trying to avoid predators
Without becoming a statistic
And learning what I was meant to.
This was a tall order
For a little tyke
But I knew given time
I would grow and prosper.
The tricky part was getting there
I was up for the challenge
But the first segment
Looked ever so daunting.
There was no better time
Than the present
So off I went
In search of that elusive shore.
For sure I was not alone
As to my left and right
There were many like myself
Trying to hide from pesky seagulls.
Which was easier said than done

But with the earth flying
In all sorts of directions
Visibility was not optimal.
I bumped into
This one and that one
I heard this swooshing noise
Then a faint cry for help.
I fell in a hole
So I scampered scurrying
This splash splished me sparingly
Next I was swimming furiously to deeper fathoms.

Eternity And A Day

The stars came down to the earth
On a sparkly, snowy night
In the morning on the ground
Was a universe of glitters.
A blanket of white crystals
Covering everything in sight
As beautiful a treasure
That was ever created.
The air was frosty cool
Slivers of ice were floating
Just drifting aimlessly
Like some ballet recital.
The clouds wore a mirror image
A reflection from top to bottom
In essence appeared two skies
Inside of one atmosphere.
So I marvelled at this wonder
In its natural splendour
Under perfect conditions
Did such a surreal vision,
So come into being
As I had to pinch myself
To make sure where I was
For such things were usually,
Only seen in one's dreams
Not in an eye opening experience
But there in all of its glory
Was a momentary resplendence.
To be held in memory

For eternity and a day
Etched in a sketch
Always vivid in my heart.
So as these twinkles
Shone from their shining
My own eyes transformed
From glimmers of glowing clusters.
As these illuminating pools
Of incandescence
Altered my complexion
By revealing underlying particles of higher perception.

Rings Which Us Encircle

The world is getting smaller
Distances are growing shorter
Life as we know it
Comes into closer contact.
For there are encounters
With higher intelligence
Which inspires a pensiveness
Towards a wider focus.
To see beyond ourselves
Or a limited comprehension
To include a totality
Not a glimpse, but the whole picture.
Then by placing these fragments
We see us in relation
To all that exists
So we start to think,
Outside of the box
By absorbing our humanity
We acknowledge our significance
Devoid of a primitive ego.
That has always held us back
From going too far forward
Yet under this atmosphere
We shed antiquated skins.
In favour of diversity
Appreciating how colours blend
Not by individual visions
But with a cosmic lens.
That encapsulates

A reverence to all latitudes
Treating all with equal measure
Not bound by a hierarchy.
But by a temporal lineage
For each horizon
Comes from a ubiquitous light
That has all along a lateral axis.
Hence all life permeates
With a glow from auspicious moons
It is our interpretation
That creates the rings which us encircle.

Different Ways

As the little girl grows
She is centered and balanced
She knows moderation
So trusts her guidance.
As a tiny soul sings
She does like a robin
So makes all of those around her
Feels as happy as a lark.
As light as a feather
As cheery as a cherry
Thankful being in her presence
For that glitter in those eyes.
Is oh so catching
It endows all near at hand
With a youthful spark
Of an exuberance.
She comes from a wish
One of sugar plums and fairies
 One so full of fun
Filled with tantalizing stories.
Her feet don't want
To touch the ground
She likes walking on air
Floating like a glistening bubble.
That keeps going higher
Upward into the beyond
From where she first came
A place of amethyst and turquoise.
Why she twinkles

From head to toe
And everywhere in between
With such an effervescence.
That streams through the air
For she's s a bundle of joy
A constant source
Of this infinite love.
For day by day
We can see for ourselves
As she reaches new heights
Touching our hearts in so many different ways.

Depths Of My Existence

When you look me in the eye
You see me through the ages
As I am, as I have been
As you peer into,
The depths of my existence
For you trace my steps
As if they were your own
So feel what I have felt.
You start to understand
That the worth of a person
Is not from what they say
But from what they do.
So you stare into my orbs
You hear and see so much more
Touching upon my very heart
Tears begin to roll down your face.
As it becomes abundantly clear
Though we come from different parts
We stand on common ground
With respect to our love of life.
For within me is music
You relate to its melody
As in you it strikes a rhythm
That is both good and kind.
So you go even farther
Each branch reveals
How their tributary
Complements as a string on a violin.
It is this merging of tones

This culmination
From an integration of rings
Which define my aura's signature.
So now you have a sense
Of what I hold dear
What inspires my soul
Why my spirit infinitely sings.
Why I'm filled with song
For this is nurturing
Why this takes to the skies
With the dawn of morning's first light.

What Is – What Isn't

Be it as this may
That our tunnel's shine
Is coming in bits and pieces
We are on an upward ascent.
We begin to open doors
To tap regions, long dormant
To use what was almost forgotten
To embrace more of ourselves.
As answers come from within
We can perceive and speak
If we only connect the dots
Which have always been there.
As we are beyond
Anything we ever thought we were
As an elucidating intuition
Has forever been at our fingertips.
This personal inquiry
Starts to show us
What we once adeptly knew
What some wanted kept secret.
Which is no longer possible
For once we initiate
By asking our spirit
What is – what isn't ?
A truth inches itself
Out of hiding
As walls so crumble
That had kept us from our purpose.
As we read this story

Which is a part of our heritage
A sentience returns
As an outline forms.
We begin to tell the difference
Between fact and fiction
By regaining an independence
That was our's in lives past.
We restore our birthright
So believe by an inner faith
Not bound by deception
Once again to be free thinkers.

Why

Why did this have to happen?
I only wanted peace
Was it too much to ask for?
Now I am an angel.
I was only a young boy
Why am I way up here?
I see my poor sister
I want her to be strong.
My mother's tears are falling
Down to a hardened earth
Please console them daddy
I will do my best from this side.
I want to touch mommy's cheek
Please let her hold me
I don't understand
Why is it like?
I'm behind a pane of glass
The sounds are all muffled
When yesterday they were clear
Does this mean that daddy and I ?
Will never again play catch
I can hear the ball
Hitting my glove
A sound that now fades,
Down an empty stretch
For I'm barefoot on some sand
I sit here listening to the waves
Touching a tranquil shore.
Please know that my spirit

Has not had its branch
Severed from our family tree
For I'll always be part of you all.
If you hear a little whistle
Gently flowing in your ears
Please be comforted
By the knowledge,
That it's just me
In my own little way
Wanting to stay as close as I can
To those I will always dearly love.

Crying At The Moon

I am at a loss
For a life so precious
Has been taken far too early
I grieve for my son's passing.
I am crying at the moon
For my heart is like its barren surface
And my spirit feels so alone
Like an iceberg drifting endlessly.
I hear an echo return
From the voice of my offspring
Down an empty corridor
Telling me the light has his past resolved.
For we all have issues
Some deal with them
Better than others
He chose to start with a clean slate.
I miss him like a forest would its trees
I think I've felt his presence
During his time of transition
I know the dogs have, by their barking.
For his residual shadow
Is still earth bound
He stands by the cedar
That reaches up to the sky.
So he begins to ascend
Higher towards an illumination
My tears replenish the roots
As he becomes its tallest branch.
My boy, my dear dear boy

You are now amongst the stars
Your sparkle will forever shine within
A chamber from which,
You shall never depart
For in me you shall remain
I will remember you fondly
Full of life and vibrant colour.
So the moon reveals an image
One that will stay constant
As will your memory
That will always be a source of happiness.

Intent And Purpose

As one door closes
The next begins to open
For as one life passes
One starts its first newborn cries.
It is in the nature
Of all that's come before
Of all that's yet to be
Under a revolving sun.
This encapsulates
Peaks, valleys and plateaus
All within a spectrum
Of undaunted, unchartered waters.
For no two are exactly the same
Yet a balancing of scales
Has such a fine clockwork precision
That day and night co-exist.
In a universal relation
Between all parts of a wheel
Creating a symmetry of horizons
Flowing smoothly from dusk to dawn.
So as light first appears
There forms a twinkling
From stars not yet invisible
That sprinkle a dust upon clouds,
Which causes dew drops to fall
In a parachuting manner
Slowly and in silence
To touch the temples,
In ardent circles

In soft, supple swirls
That gently and gingerly
Affect widening apertures.
For it is by this movement
Which alters one's climate
To clear away mists
In which a focus is ever present.
So a wind speaks of cleansing
An eagle acts as a messenger
As time no longer stands still
It moves forth with intent and purpose.

Unforgiving

Two ships passing in the night
Barely aware
Of the other's existence
If not for sounds,
On an open breeze
Voices carried over water
Have a magnifying effect
Across all distances.
Emblems etched on flags
Details one's origins
Where they are from
The land of their mother tongue.
Lakes which accommodate
Such steel mammoths
On exchanges of commerce
Attending ports of trade.
But it's their silent surges
In displacement of tides
Which propel them along
To reach these destinations.
In the midst of a mist
Of a deceiving fog
That blasts from a horn
So shatter a quietness.
All to avoid
Any sad mishaps
Where collisions of this type
Shake a sea to its bare bones.
Then to lie dormant

At the very bottom
Where they used to
Peer down under.
More than a humbling demise
The shock from a
Colossal crack
Sending the mighty,
To the consoling meek
To sit on an unforgiving
Dark and dreary resting place
Best to be heard to stay unblemished.

Wisp Of Air

Your words have found a means
To reach those destined
To strike a chord
Which so resonates.
As a breeze was guided down
To work its magic
To bring thoughts stuck
Inside of a book,
Out into the open
To breathe a purpose
To realize a premonition
By an insightful exhalation.
As a cover forever still
Had its pages revealed
To come to the exact spot
Where they were meant to be.
To have such density
A bearing on one's direction
To provide the nudge
A necessary slight push.
It's a small miracle
For how can you describe ?
This liberation
The loosening of a rigidness.
There's just no quit in you
No matter the hurdles
You kept the principles
That code of beliefs.
So stayed a course

Through the dry spells
Endured the countless
Crumpled pieces of paper.
Those eyes would not close
Propped them up at times
But you held on
With all that you had.
Then came a wisp of air
As faint as it was
This was the initial
Which lead to fulfillment.

Silence Of Its Sound

There was an anomaly
In earth's gravitational field
A short duration window
In a re-alignment of balance.
You could place a broom
In the center of a room
And it would stay upright
All on its own.
Defying the known laws
To expect it to fall over
There it was straight
Up and down, not laying flat.
A magical moment
A realm inside a realm
The air around
Tingled with sparkles.
As in a chamber
That held these properties
Went against the grain
Resetting the templates.
As going forward
Was the very same
To coming back
To where we once were.
It just felt different
A momentary transition
But one that did merge
With our meridians.
And then it was gone

As the moon dips in the sky
Traipsing off to another place
To make its presence felt.
Not left empty handed
And so forever changed
By such an experience
Having shared this exposure.
The eyes adjusted
To this stimulus
Breaking new ground
Absorbing the silence of its sound.

Fire With Fire

The world has not always
Been your oyster
But this adversity
Has been your building blocks.
As you have strengthened
By each challenge
For you put your heart and soul
Into each step you take.
At times we may fall
Just as fast you
Spring right back up
Dusting off your hands.
As you expected
To have a time of it
To struggle as you will
To show some wear and tear.
This creates character
A solid base
From which so forms
Auspicious beginnings.
Never got the better of you
So kept up the faith
Throughout all the turmoil
In some doubting dark hours.
You did not lose face
As daunting as it was
You failed to acquiesce
To a coercive force.
Met fire with fire

Didn't back down
Your spine served you well
Finding a few bright spots.
It was this perception
Why others in
Your same situation
Were enveloped by despair.
Just look at you now
You took a burden
Turned it inside out
From a negative to prosperity.

Coat Of Arms

A distinguished life
An honourable career
Altruistic to the core
To help in any,
Way that he could
For a town named
After his bloodline
So proud was this man.
To lessen one's pains
To bring a smile
Time was no consequence
Just the wellbeing,
Of his fellow person
To touch the lives
With those he felt kinship
Regardless of name,
Or their station
So shared what he had
Was the better man for it
This soul of generosity.
As he was of the opinion
That if you had privilege
This was not to be abused
But to be a means,
To lift them up
From ever they were
To restore their dignity
In a respectful manner.
Such was his stature

Beloved by a people
A born leader
A heart amongst hearts.
So when this ville
Created its coat of arms
A feather was etched
From an adored plumage.
To represent
To mark as a kindness
One who had always shown others
A love amongst loves.

Vincelles

The pride in your name
Its origins
Your family history
What they were known for.
Most were wine producers
All were benefactors
Who wanted to give back
As a sign of gratitude.
A time when one's word
Meant what it said
As those pulled together
As the symbol,
Of a woven sinew
That was indivisible
As thoughts centered around
A single tree.
From which all so came
Circles of heredity
A provenance
In the ville of Vincelles.
There was no question
As to the testimony
Of an inner ring
Whose flame burned brightly.
Footsteps remembered
As a legacy
For those to come
Of the shoes they would fill.
Plaques still to this day

Etch good deeds done
Though long departed
Yet near in heart.
A character
In these defined
A strength that ran
Through and evenly through.
In a land of the Romantics
Waters as pure
Souls as vibrant
As their uncommon nature.

Incessant Burning

The fires are raging
The trees are crumbling
The smoke in this haze
Is a crimson termination.
All is tinder dry
Slight change in wind direction
Can be the difference
Between life and death.
This incessant burning
Hisses like a snake
Even they are in peril
Our beloved koala bears.
To the point of extinction
From a glistening blade
Warnings fallen on deaf ears
Until they too are in its path.
This scorching sharpness
Has us at its mercy
Those who have come from abroad
We owe a debt of gratitude.
Is there relief ?
A brief shower
A cooling period
A silent breeze.
This has been relentless
The skies overhead
So blackened out
By this choking nemesis.
Nowhere to turn

Forced to the shores
By this creeping crawler
That singes searingly.
A national tragedy
A doomsday prophecy
One we wish to extinguish
By any means possible.
So hard to breathe
Lungs like a desert
Throats by embers parched
Will there be a tomorrow ?